MACBETH

William Shakespeare

Abridged and adapted by Emily Hutchinson

Illustrated by Steve Moore

A PACEMAKER CLASSIC

GLOBE FEARON

Pearson Learning Group

Executive Editor: Joan Carrafiello
Project Editor: Karen Bernhaut
Editorial Assistant: Keisha Carter
Production Director: Penny Gibson
Print Buyer: Cheryl Johnson
Production Editor: Alan Dalgleish
Desktop Specialist: Margarita T. Linnartz
Art Direction: Joan Jacobus
Marketing Manager: Marge Curson
Cover and Interior Illustrations: Steve Moore
Cover Design: Margarita T. Linnartz

ISBN 0-835-91232-9
Printed in the United States of America

11 12 13 14 15   10 09 08 07 06

Globe
Fearon

Pearson Learning Group

1-800-321-3106
www.pearsonlearning.com

Contents

Cast of Characters

DUNCAN   The King of Scotland, a good and hon-
                          est man. He is murdered by Macbeth.

MACBETH   A Scottish thane (nobleman) and a
                          general in Duncan's army.

LADY MACBETH   Macbeth's wife.

BANQUO   A friend of Macbeth's. He is murdered
                          when he is seen as a threat.

FLEANCE   Banquo's son. He escapes when his
                          father is murdered.

MALCOLM   Son of Duncan and heir to the throne.
                          He flees Scotland after Duncan's
                          death.

DONALBAIN   Another son of Duncan. He also flees
                          Scotland after Duncan's death.

MACDUFF   A thane and a general in Duncan's
                          army. He cares about the good of
                          Scotland.

LADY MACDUFF   Macduff's wife. Macbeth orders her
                          and her family killed.

ROSS   Macduff's cousin.

LENNOX   A thane, loyal to Duncan.

SEYTON   Macbeth's aide.

SIWARD   An English earl who helps Malcolm.

YOUNG SIWARD   Siward's son. He bravely faces
                          Macbeth in battle and is killed.

THE THREE WITCHES   Supernatural beings who tell Macbeth
                          and Banquo the future.

Act 1

Near a battlefield in Scotland, three witches meet during a storm. They agree to meet again, after the battle. They plan to greet Macbeth before sunset.

Meanwhile, a sergeant reports to Duncan about the battle. To reward Macbeth for his brave acts on the field, Duncan decides to give him the title of thane of Cawdor. That evening, the three witches greet Macbeth by this title and tell him that he will soon be king.

Later, Duncan, his sons Malcolm and Donalbain, Banquo, and other lords visit Inverness, Macbeth's castle. Lady Macbeth, wanting to be queen, encourages her husband to kill King Duncan.

Scene 1

Thunder and lightning. Three WITCHES *enter.*

WITCH 1: When shall we three meet again?
    In thunder, lightning, or in rain?

WITCH 2: When the hurlyburly's done.
    When the battle is lost and won.

WITCH 3: That will be
    Before sunset tonight.

WITCH 1: Where shall we meet?

WITCH 2: Upon the heath.

WITCH 3: There we shall meet Macbeth.

ALL: Fair is foul, and foul is fair.
    Hover through the fog and filthy air.

(*The* WITCHES *exit.*)

Scene 2

A camp near Forres, Scotland. KING DUNCAN, MALCOLM, DONALBAIN, LENNOX, *attendants, and a wounded* SERGEANT *enter.*

DUNCAN: Who is that bleeding man?
    Perhaps he can tell us
    How the battle is going.

MALCOLM: This is the sergeant
    Who, like a good and strong soldier,
    Fought to save me from being captured.
    Greetings, brave friend!
    Tell the king how the battle is going.

SERGEANT: At first it was hard to tell
    Which side was winning. It seemed like
    Two tired swimmers clinging together,
    Each one drowning the other.
    All his evil deeds led Macdonwald,
    That rebel, to this moment.
    Luck was on his side for a time.
    But Macdonwald and luck together
    Were not strong enough to fight Macbeth.
    With his sword, Macbeth carved his way
    Through the battle until he faced the rebel.
    Macbeth did not leave the battlefield
    Until he had ripped Macdonwald open
    From his belly to his jaws
    And displayed his head on a stick.

DUNCAN: Oh, brave cousin!
    Worthy warrior!

SERGEANT: But no sooner had Macbeth
　　　Done these brave deeds than new danger
　　　Came from the east.
　　　Listen, king of Scotland! Listen!
　　　As soon as Macdonwald's troops ran away,
　　　The Norwegian lord thought
　　　He saw his chance.
　　　With new supplies of men,
　　　He began a fresh attack.

DUNCAN: Did this not dismay
　　　Our captains, Macbeth and Banquo?

SERGEANT: Yes, of course.
　　　About as much as sparrows dismay eagles,
　　　Or rabbits dismay lions.
　　　The truth is that Macbeth and Banquo were
　　　Like cannons loaded with double charges.
　　　For every stroke of the enemy,
　　　They gave back four.
　　　But I am faint. My gashes cry for help.

DUNCAN: Your words and your wounds
　　　Have something in common.
　　　They both tell of honor.
　　　(*to attendant*) Take him to the surgeons.

(SERGEANT *exits, with attendant.* ROSS *enters.*)

ROSS: Your Majesty, we come from Fife,
　　　Where the Norwegian flags fly
　　　And make our people cold with fear.
　　　The king of Norway himself,
　　　With great numbers of troops,
　　　Was helped by the thane of Cawdor.

But then along came Macbeth,
And showed him who was stronger.
After a long and difficult battle,
The victory fell on us.

DUNCAN: Great happiness!
Never again shall that traitor,
The thane of Cawdor, betray us.
He shall be executed right away.
Go and announce that he is dead.
Then greet Macbeth with his former title.

ROSS: I'll make sure it is done.

DUNCAN: What Cawdor has lost,
Noble Macbeth has won.

(*All exit.*)

Scene 3

Near Forres. Thunder. The WITCHES *enter.*

WITCH 1: Where have you been, sister?

WITCH 2: I was doing plenty of mischief.

WITCH 3: Sister, where were you?

WITCH 1: I was doing the same.

(*A drum sounds.*)

WITCH 3: A drum, a drum!
Macbeth has come!

(MACBETH *and* BANQUO *enter.*)

MACBETH: So foul and fair a day
I have never seen before.

BANQUO: How far is it to Forres?
(*He sees the* WITCHES.)

What are these, so withered and so wild?
They do not look as if they belong on earth.
(*To the* WITCHES) Are you alive?
You look something like women,
But your beards make you seem otherwise.

MACBETH: Speak, if you can.
What are you?

WITCH 1: All hail, Macbeth!
Hail to you, thane of Glamis!

WITCH 2: All hail, Macbeth!
Hail to you, thane of Cawdor!

WITCH 3: All hail, Macbeth!
You shall soon be king!

BANQUO (*to* MACBETH): Good sir,
Why do you look as if you fear
Things that do sound so fair? *good*
(*to* WITCHES) In the name of truth,
Are you creatures of our imagination?
You greet my noble friend with the title
He now has. But you also greet him with
Another title that he does not have.
Then you tell him he will soon be king.
Yet you do not speak to me.
If you can look into the future,
Then tell me mine.

WITCHES: Hail!

WITCH 1: You are less than Macbeth,
And greater.

WITCH 2: You are not as happy
As Macbeth, yet much happier.

WITCH 3: Your sons shall be kings, *Banquo*
    Even though you shall not.

WITCHES: Banquo and Macbeth, all hail!

MACBETH: Stay, you speakers of riddles.
    Tell me more.
    I already know that I am thane of Glamis.
    But why do you call me thane of Cawdor?
    The thane of Cawdor still lives,
    And to be king is no more possible
    Than to be thane of Cawdor.
    Tell me where
    You got this strange information.
    Speak, I command you.

(WITCHES *vanish.*)

BANQUO: The earth has bubbles,
    Just as the water does. These creatures
    Have vanished just like bubbles.
    Where have they gone?

MACBETH: Into the air.
    What seemed like bodies has melted
    Like breath into the wind.

BANQUO: Were they really here?
    Or were we mad for a moment?

MACBETH: Your sons shall be kings.

BANQUO: You shall be king.

MACBETH: And thane of Cawdor, too.
    Wasn't that what they said?

BANQUO: That is exactly what they said.

(ROSS *and* ANGUS *enter.*)

ROSS: The king has happily received
　　News of your success, Macbeth.

ANGUS: We have been sent by the king
　　To thank you for what you did.

ROSS: As an advance payment
　　For what you did on the battlefield,
　　He told us to call you thane of Cawdor.
　　So we say, hail, most worthy thane!

BANQUO (*aside*): What?
　　Did the witches tell the truth?

MACBETH (*aside*): Thane of Glamis,
　　And thane of Cawdor!
　　The best is yet to come!
　　(*to* ROSS *and* ANGUS)
　　Thank you, gentlemen,
　　For bringing this news.
　　(*to* BANQUO) Do you not hope that
　　Your sons shall be kings?
　　Those who told me I would have the title
　　Of thane of Cawdor
　　Promised no less to them.

BANQUO: It is strange. But sometimes,
　　The powers of evil tell us things
　　To win our souls.
　　They give us small favors
　　And later betray us in important matters.

MACBETH (*aside*): They told two truths—
　　They called me thane of Glamis
　　And thane of Cawdor.
　　These titles are nothing compared to king.

The witches' words might be false,
Or they might be true. Yet, if they are false,
Why is there some truth in them?
After all, I am now thane of Cawdor.
If their words are true, why am I thinking
About something that makes my heart
Knock at my ribs? I can be king
Only if King Duncan is dead.
The idea of killing Duncan is horrible.
It goes against nature. Yet I cannot stop
Thinking about wearing the crown.

BANQUO: Look at Macbeth.
He seems to be in a trance.

MACBETH (*aside*): If my fate is to be king,
Then chance may crown me.
Perhaps I do not have to do anything.

BANQUO: New honors come upon Macbeth
Like new clothing. They will fit better
After they have been used for a while.

MACBETH (*aside*): Come what may,
There is an end to even the hardest day.

BANQUO: Worthy Macbeth, we are waiting
For you to say something.

MACBETH: Forgive me. My dull brain was
Disturbed by things I had forgotten.
Let us now go to see the king.
(*to* BANQUO) Think about today's events.
Later, when we have more time,
Let us speak our free and open minds
To each other.

BANQUO (*to* MACBETH): Gladly.

MACBETH (*to* BANQUO): Till then.
(*to* ROSS *and* ANGUS) Come, friends.

(*All exit.*)

Scene 4

The palace at Forres. KING DUNCAN, MALCOLM,
DONALBAIN, LENNOX, *and attendants enter.*

DUNCAN: Has Cawdor been executed yet?

MALCOLM: My lord, I spoke to someone
Who saw him die. He reported that
Cawdor confessed that he was a traitor.
He then begged for your forgiveness,
Saying he was very sorry.
Nothing in his life
Became him like the leaving of it. He died
As one who had trained himself for death.
He seemed to throw away
The dearest thing he owned
As if it meant nothing to him.

DUNCAN: There is no way
To read someone's thoughts in the face.
I thought he was a gentleman
Whom I could trust.
(MACBETH, BANQUO, ROSS, *and* ANGUS *enter.*)
Macbeth! Worthy cousin!
I owe you more than I can ever pay!

MACBETH: On the contrary!
Keeping you safe is payment in itself.

10

DUNCAN: Welcome, Macbeth!
 And noble Banquo! Welcome to you!
 Your services shall also be rewarded.
 I would like to take this opportunity
 To name my son Malcolm
 The prince of Cumberland.
 He is now the official heir to the throne.
 For now, let us go to Inverness,
 Macbeth's castle. We all need to rest.

MACBETH: I shall go ahead of all of you.
 I will tell my wife that you are coming.
 Farewell for now.
 (*Aside*) The prince of Cumberland!
 That is a step on which I must fall down,
 Or else leap over, for in my way it lies.
 Stars, hide your fires.
 Do not let light shine on my dark desires.

DUNCAN: Worthy Banquo,
 Macbeth is generous, brave, and noble.
 Let us follow him to Inverness, his home.

(*All exit.*)

Scene 5

Inverness. Macbeth's castle. LADY MACBETH *enters, with a letter.*

LADY MACBETH: My husband's letter
 Tells about his meeting with three witches.
 They called him thane of Glamis,
 Which he is. Then, thane of Cawdor,
 Which he soon became. He shall be

What he was promised—the king!
Yet I fear his nature is
Too full of the milk of human kindness
To do what must be done.
He has enough ambition, but he does not
Have enough evil to go with it.
What he wants, he wants it to be holy.
He does not want to be false to anyone,
And yet he wants to win. Come home,
My husband, so that I may speak to you.
I will tell you what you must do
To get what you want.
(*A* MESSENGER *enters.*) What is it?

MESSENGER: The king comes here tonight.

LADY MACBETH: You are mad to say it!
My husband would have told me about it
So I could prepare.

MESSENGER: It is true.
Lord Macbeth is on his way.
He sent a messenger ahead of him.
Almost dead for breath, he had enough
To give me the message.

LADY MACBETH: Take care of him.
He brings great news.
(MESSENGER *exits.*) Come, you spirits
That guide evil thoughts of murder.
Help me here. Fill me from head to toe
With cruel thoughts! Make my blood thick.
Stop up all thoughts of being sorry.
Let no weak feelings stop me!

Come to me, thick night.
Do not let heaven peep through the
Blanket of the dark
To cry, "Stop, stop!"
(MACBETH *enters.*)
Great Glamis! Worthy Cawdor!
Greater than both! You are king!
Your letter has taken me from
The present moment.
I now feel the future has arrived.

MACBETH: My dearest love,
Duncan comes here tonight.

LADY MACBETH: And when does he leave?

MACBETH: Tomorrow, he says.

LADY MACBETH: Oh, never
Shall he see the sun again.
Your face, my dear, is like a book.
It is easy to read. To fool the world,
You must learn to act a little bit.
Welcome Duncan with your eyes,
Your hands, and your words.
Look like the innocent flower,
But be the snake hiding under it.
Leave this night's business to me.

MACBETH: We will speak some more.

LADY MACBETH: Keep your goals clear.
To change your mind would lead to fear.
Leave all the rest to me.

(MACBETH *and* LADY MACBETH *exit.*)

Scene 6

In front of Macbeth's castle. KING DUNCAN, MALCOLM, DONALBAIN, BANQUO, LENNOX, MACDUFF, ROSS, ANGUS, *and attendants enter.*

DUNCAN: This castle is very pleasant.
    The air feels sweet to our senses.

BANQUO: I see that a summer bird
    Likes it here, too. Where the martin
    Makes its nest, I have noticed that
    The air is delicate.

(LADY MACBETH *enters.*)

DUNCAN: See, see!
    Here is our honored hostess!
    We thank you for your trouble.

LADY MACBETH: Whatever we can do
    For you, we shall consider an honor.

DUNCAN: Where is the thane of Cawdor?
    We followed right behind him,
    But he was fast. His great love for you
    Sped him home before we could catch up.
    Fair and noble hostess,
    We are your guests tonight.
    Give me your hand.
    Take me to your husband.
    We are looking forward to seeing him.

(*All exit.*)

Scene 7

Inside Macbeth's castle. MACBETH *enters.*

MACBETH: If it must be done, then it is best
That it be done quickly. But it is not easy.
He is here in my home, and he trusts me.
I am not only his cousin,
I am also his subject.
Both of these facts argue against the deed.
As his host, I should shut the door
Against any murderer.
I should not carry the knife myself.
Besides, this Duncan has always
Been good to me.
I have no reason to kill him, other than
My own wish to be king.
(LADY MACBETH *enters.*)
What news do you have?

LADY MACBETH: He is almost done eating.
Why did you leave the room?

MACBETH: Has he asked for me?

LADY MACBETH: Of course he has.

MACBETH: We will go no further
In this business. He has honored me
By making me thane of Cawdor.
I should enjoy this honor,
And not cast it aside so soon.

LADY MACBETH: What about your hopes?
Have they gone to sleep? Are you afraid
To be the same in your actions

As you are in your desires?
Would you live as a coward
In your own eyes? Would you let
"I dare not" stand in the way of "I would"?
Are you like the cat who wanted the fish
But did not want to get its feet wet?

MACBETH: Please, stop!
I dare to do all that a man can do.
Whoever does more than that is not a man.

LADY MACBETH: What beast was it, then,
That made you even bring this up?
What kind of a man are you,
To talk of this, and then change your mind?

MACBETH: What if we should fail?

LADY MACBETH: Fail? Keep your courage,
And we shall not fail.
When Duncan is asleep,
I will give his guards wine and brandy.
Soon, they will fall into deep sleeps, too.
Then, we can do what we like to Duncan.
We can even make it look as if
His own guards had done it.

MACBETH: After we have used the daggers
Belonging to the guards, we will smear
The guards with Duncan's blood.
Everyone will think they did it!

LADY MACBETH: Who would dare say
Anything else? Especially when we will
Appear to be mourning Duncan's death?

MACBETH: So be it! My mind is made up.
　　Let's get on with it.
　　We will put on a good show.
　　False face must hide what
　　The false heart will know.
(MACBETH *and* LADY MACBETH *exit.*)

Act 2

Macbeth kills Duncan, and Lady Macbeth smears the drugged and sleeping guards with blood. Macduff and Lennox arrive at Inverness, wishing to see Duncan. They discover the body and wake the entire house.

Macbeth kills the guards, blaming Duncan's death on them. Duncan's sons flee, Malcolm to England and Donalbain to Ireland.
Ross and Macduff decide that Duncan's sons had paid the guards to kill their father.

Scene 1

The courtyard of Macbeth's castle. BANQUO *and* FLEANCE *enter.*

BANQUO: What time is it, son?

FLEANCE: The moon is down.
    I have not heard the clock.

BANQUO: The moon goes down
    At midnight.

FLEANCE: Then it must be after twelve, sir.

BANQUO: Here, hold my sword and dagger.
    The heavens must be saving energy.
    All the stars have gone out.
    I am so tired. Yet I do not wish to sleep.
    I am afraid of the bad dreams I might have.
    (MACBETH *and a servant enter.*)
    Give me back my sword, son.
    Who's there?

MACBETH: A friend.

BANQUO: What, sir, not yet at rest?
   The king is asleep.
   After enjoying your kind hospitality,
   He went to bed, very content.

MACBETH: Too bad we were not prepared.
   We were not able to do as much for him
   As we would have liked to.

BANQUO: Everything turned out fine.
   I dreamed last night
   Of the three Weird Sisters.
   Some of what they told you has come true.

MACBETH: I haven't even thought of them.
   Yet when we can find the time,
   Let's talk about that business.

BANQUO: Whenever you'd like.

MACBETH: I hope you will support me
   When the time comes.

BANQUO: Of course I will,
   If I can do so in good conscience.

MACBETH: Sleep well!

BANQUO: Thank you, sir. The same to you!

(BANQUO *and* FLEANCE *exit.*)

MACBETH (*to servant*): Go tell my wife
   To ring the bell when my drink is ready.
   (*Servant exits.*)
   Is this a dagger which I see before me,
   The handle toward my hand?
   Come, let me hold you. I cannot touch you,

And yet I can see you.
Fatal vision, are you something
That can only be seen but not touched?
Are you but a dagger of the mind,
A false creation of my brain?
I see you, in a form that seems real.
You remind me of my plan
And of the weapon I was going to use.
Either my eyes are deceiving me,
Or they are sharper than my other senses.
I can still see you, and on your blade
I see blood that was not there before.
There's no such thing. I'm just imagining it.
(*He begins to walk to* DUNCAN's *room.*)
Firm earth, hear not my steps.
Do not notice which way they walk.
I fear the very stones tell where I am.
(*A bell rings.*) Ah, the bell!
My wife's signal that it is time!
Do not hear it, Duncan. It is a sound
That means you'll soon be in the ground.

(MACBETH *exits.*)

Scene 2

The castle hall. LADY MACBETH *enters.*

LADY MACBETH: The drink that
Made the guards drunk has made me bold.
What put them to sleep has given me fire.
(*An owl hoots.*) What was that?
It was just an owl shrieking.
Macbeth must be in Duncan's room now.
The doors are open,

And the guards are sound asleep.
He should have no trouble.

(MACBETH *enters.*)

MACBETH: Who's there? Oh, it's you!

LADY MACBETH: You're back so soon!
I'm afraid it did not go well.
Did the guards wake up?
I should have done it myself
When I was there.
If Duncan had not reminded me of
My own father as he slept,
I would have done it.
What happened, my husband?

MACBETH: I have done the deed.
Did you hear any noise?

LADY MACBETH: Just an owl screaming.

MACBETH: Who sleeps in the other room?

LADY MACBETH: Malcolm and Donalbain. *King Duncan's*

MACBETH (*looking at his bloody hands*): *Son*
This is a sorry sight.

LADY MACBETH: Don't be a fool.

MACBETH: Someone laughed in his sleep.
Another one cried, "Murder!"
They were in another room, near Duncan's.
They woke each other up.
I heard them as they said some prayers.
One cried, "God bless us!"
The other said, "Amen."
As I stood there with my bloody hands,
I could not say "Amen" with them.

LADY MACBETH: Stop thinking about it.

MACBETH: But why couldn't I say "Amen,"
   When the other had said "God bless us?"
   I had great need of blessing, and "Amen"
   Stuck in my throat.

LADY MACBETH: These deeds must not
   Be thought of in these ways. If we do so,
   It will make us mad.

MACBETH: I thought I heard a voice cry,
   "Sleep no more!
   Macbeth does murder sleep."
   The innocent sleep, sleep that knits up
   The raveled sleeve of care.
   Sleep—the death of each day's life.

LADY MACBETH: What are you saying?

MACBETH: Then the voice cried,
   "Sleep no more!" to all the house.
   "Macbeth has murdered a sleeping man,
   And so Macbeth shall sleep no more."

LADY MACBETH: Who said this?
   My husband, you weaken yourself
   By thinking such mad thoughts.
   Go get some water
   And wash the blood from your hands.
   And why did you bring these daggers?
   They must lie there. Put them back,
   And smear the sleeping guards with blood.

MACBETH: I will not go back there.
   I'm afraid to think about what I have done.
   I dare not look at it again.

LADY MACBETH: You are too weak!
 Give me the daggers.
 The sleeping and the dead are like pictures.
 Only a child fears a painting of evil.
 I'll smear the faces of the guards
 With Duncan's blood.
 That will make them look guilty.

Quote

(LADY MACBETH *exits. A knocking from within.*)

MACBETH: What is that knocking?
 Why is it that every noise frightens me?
 What hands are here? Ha!
 They pluck out my eyes.
 Will all the oceans wash this blood
 Clean from my hand? No! Instead,
 My hands will make the vast seas red.

(LADY MACBETH *enters again.*)

LADY MACBETH: My hands are now
 As red as yours. But I am ashamed
 That my heart is white with fear.
 (*More knocking*) I hear a knocking
 At the south gate. Let us go to our room.
 A little water clears us of this deed.
 How easy is it then! You lost your nerve
 For a minute. (*More knocking*) Listen!
 More knocking. Put your robe on,
 So it will not look as if we've been awake.
 Stop thinking about it. Try to act normal.

MACBETH: Because of what I've just done,
 I cannot bear to know my own thoughts.
 (*More knocking*)

Wake Duncan with your knocking!
I wish you could!

(MACBETH *and* LADY MACBETH *exit.*)

Scene 3

The courtyard of the castle. A PORTER *enters. More knocking.*

PORTER: Who's there? Stop knocking!
You'll wake up the whole house!
I'm on my way!

(The PORTER *opens the gate.* MACDUFF *and* LENNOX *enter.)*

MACDUFF: Did you get to bed late, friend?
Is that why it was so difficult for you
To get up and answer our knocking?

PORTER: Yes, sir. We were up drinking
Until after two o'clock this morning.

MACDUFF: Is your master awake?
(MACBETH *enters.*) Ah, I see that he is.
Our knocking woke him up, too.

LENNOX: Good morning, noble sir.

MACBETH: Good morning to you both.

MACDUFF: Is King Duncan awake?

MACBETH: Not yet.

MACDUFF: He asked me to wake him early.
I had almost missed the time we agreed on.

MACBETH: I'll bring you to him.

MACDUFF: I'm sorry for the trouble.

MACBETH: No trouble at all.
　　Here is the door.

MACDUFF: I'll just go in.
　　I know that King Duncan is expecting me.

(MACDUFF *exits.*)

LENNOX: Is the king leaving today?

MACBETH: Yes. He has arranged for it.

LENNOX: It has been an unusual night.
　　It was very windy, and some people said
　　That they heard strange screams of death.
　　The owl was shrieking all night.
　　Some said the earth itself was shaking.

MACBETH: Yes, it was a rough night.

LENNOX: I cannot remember
　　Another one like it.

(MACDUFF *enters again.*)

MACDUFF: Oh, horror, horror, horror!
　　Neither tongue nor heart can name it!

MACBETH *and* LENNOX: What is it?

MACDUFF: The most terrible murder
　　Has taken the life of the king!

MACBETH: What are you saying?

LENNOX: Is King Duncan dead?

MACDUFF: Look in his room.
　　See for yourself. Do not ask me to speak.
　　See, and then speak yourselves.
　　(MACBETH *and* LENNOX *exit.*)

Awake, awake!
Ring the alarm bells. Murder and treason!
Banquo and Donalbain! Malcolm! Awake!
Shake off sleep, which looks like death,
And look on death itself! Up, up, and see
What has happened! Malcolm! Banquo!
Rise up from your beds,
And see this horror! Ring the bell!

(*Bell rings.* LADY MACBETH *enters.*)

LADY MACBETH: What is happening?
Why are you making so much noise?
You'll wake everyone in the house!

MACDUFF: Oh, gentle lady,
It is not something you want to hear.
Such words as I would speak
Would kill a woman, if she heard them.
(BANQUO *enters.*) Oh, Banquo, Banquo,
Our royal master has been murdered!

LADY MACBETH: Oh, woe! Alas!
What, in our house?

BANQUO: Dear Macduff, please,
Say it is not so.

(MACBETH, LENNOX, *and* ROSS *enter.*)

MACBETH: If I had died an hour ago,
I would have lived a good life.
From this moment on, nothing in my life
Is important. All is but toys.
Honor and grace are dead.
The wine of life has all been poured.
Only the bitter drops are left.

(MALCOLM *and* DONALBAIN *enter.*)

DONALBAIN: What is wrong?

MACBETH: A terrible thing has happened.
    The fountain of your own blood is stopped.
    The source of your life has ended.

MACDUFF: Your father has been murdered.

MALCOLM: Who did it?

LENNOX: His own guards did it.
    Their hands and faces were smeared
    With blood. So were their daggers.
    No man's life was to be trusted with them.

MACBETH: I was so angry,
    That I killed them both.

MACDUFF: Why did you do that?

MACBETH: I couldn't help it.   *angry*
    Who can be wise, amazed, furious, loyal,
    And calm, all at the same time? No man.
    My love for Duncan took over!
    Here lay Duncan, his silver skin
    Covered with his golden blood.
    There lay the murderers,
    Covered with the colors of their crime.
    Their daggers were dripping with blood.
    Who could have stopped from killing them?

LADY MACBETH: Help me!
    I think I'm going to faint!

(LADY MACBETH *faints.*)

MACDUFF: Help the lady.

29

MALCOLM (*aside to* DONALBAIN): I think
You and I might be in danger.

DONALBAIN (*aside to* MALCOLM):
We should probably get away from here.
We will cry for our father later.

BANQUO: Take care of the lady.
(LADY MACBETH *is carried out.*)
Let us all change from our night clothes.
After we are dressed, let us meet
And talk about this most bloody
Piece of work, to understand it better.
Together, we must decide what to do.

MACBETH: Let's all meet in the hall later.

(All but MALCOLM *and* DONALBAIN *exit.*)

MALCOLM: Let's not meet with them.
I'll go to England. What will you do?

DONALBAIN: I'll go to Ireland.
It would be best for us not to be together.
That way, each of us will be safer.
Where we are, there are daggers
In men's smiles.
The closer a man is related to us,
The more likely he would kill us
To get the crown.

MALCOLM: I have a feeling that the killing
Is not yet over. The arrow that's been shot
Has not yet landed. Our safest plan
Is to stay out of its way.
Therefore, let's get on our horses.

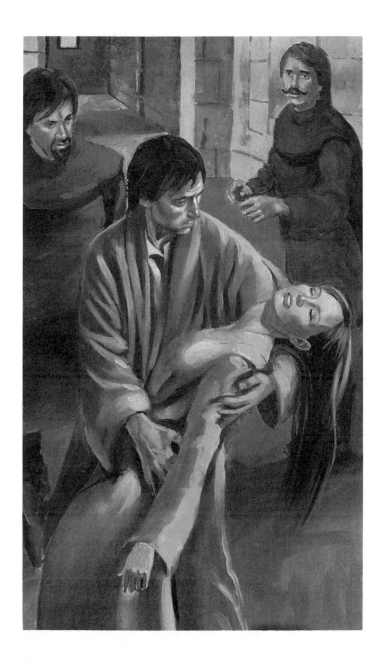

31

We won't even say good-bye to anyone.
We'll just leave. It's our best chance.

Scene 4

Outside Macbeth's castle. ROSS *and an* OLD MAN
enter.

OLD MAN: In my long life of 70 years,
I have never seen a time like this.
So many things have happened
That are not natural.

ROSS: Yes. The clock says it is day,
But the sun has not come out yet.

OLD MAN: Not only that, but I heard
About a falcon who was killed by an owl.

ROSS: Did you hear that Duncan's horses
Turned wild and broke out of their stalls?

OLD MAN: I heard that they ate each other.

ROSS: They did, to my amazement. I saw it
With my own eyes. (MACDUFF *enters.*)
Here comes the good Macduff.
How goes the world now, sir?

MACDUFF: Can't you see?
It's still dark, when it should be light.

ROSS: Who killed King Duncan?

MACDUFF: The guards that Macbeth killed.

ROSS: Why did they do it?

MACDUFF: They must have been paid.
Malcolm and Donalbain, the king's sons,

Have run away. This makes them
Look guilty, don't you think?

ROSS: What a terrible crime —
To kill their own father! Then it is likely
That Macbeth will be the next king.

MACDUFF: He's already been named king.
He has gone to Scone to be crowned.

ROSS: Where is Duncan's body?

MACDUFF: It has been taken to Colmekill,
The sacred burial ground of our kings.

ROSS: Will you go to Scone?

MACDUFF: No, I'll go home to Fife.

OLD MAN: May God's blessings go
With both of you.

(*All exit.*)

Act 3

Banquo thinks about what the witches had said. He realizes that all their words about Macbeth have come true. He suspects Macbeth of foul play, and he remembers the witches' words about his own sons.

Macbeth arranges to have Banquo and Fleance killed. Fleance escapes as Banquo is murdered. That evening, Macbeth and Lady Macbeth, as king and queen, welcome guests to a banquet. As everyone sits down, Macbeth sees a vision of Banquo's ghost. He speaks to it in such a way that his part in Banquo's death becomes clear. Lady Macbeth orders the guests to leave, saying that her husband is not himself.

Suspicious of Macbeth, Macduff goes to England. His plan is to get help from King Edward against Macbeth.

Scene 1

The palace at Forres. BANQUO *enters.*

BANQUO: Everything the witches said
　　Has come true. Macbeth is king now.
　　I fear he got there through foul play.
　　But didn't they also say that I myself
　　Would be the father of many kings?
　　If they told the truth to him, then
　　They probably told the truth to me.
　　But there's no point in thinking about it.

(*Trumpets sound.* MACBETH, *now the king, enters, followed by* LADY MACBETH, LENNOX, ROSS, *lords, and attendants.*)

MACBETH (*to* BANQUO): There you are,
    Our most important guest.

LADY MACBETH: If Banquo had not come
    It would have ruined our party!

MACBETH: Tonight is a big feast,
    And I hope you'll be there.

BANQUO: Of course, your Highness.
    It would be an honor and a pleasure.

MACBETH: Are you riding this afternoon?

BANQUO: Yes, my good lord.

MACBETH: I had hoped to spend some time
    With you this afternoon. But tomorrow
    Will be just as well. Will you be riding far?

BANQUO: Far enough to fill the time
    Between now and supper. I should be back
    About an hour after dark.

MACBETH: Do not miss our feast.

BANQUO: My lord, I will not.

MACBETH: You know, our bloody cousins,
    Malcolm and Donalbain,
    Are in England and in Ireland.
    They have not confessed their cruel crime.
    Instead, they make up strange stories.
    But we'll talk about that tomorrow.
    Go for your ride. We'll see you tonight.
    Is Fleance going with you?

BANQUO: Yes, my good lord.

MACBETH: May your horses be swift
And sure of foot. Farewell until tonight.
(BANQUO *exits*.)
Let every man do as he pleases
Until seven at night.
We shall all meet again for supper.
(*All exit, except* MACBETH *and a* SERVANT.)
I asked to see some men.
Did they arrive yet?

SERVANT: Yes, my lord.
They are waiting by the palace gate.

MACBETH: Show them in.
(SERVANT *exits*.) To have the title of king
Means nothing unless I have it safely.
I don't trust Banquo. He has many qualities
That should be feared. He is brave,
And he is wise enough to act in safety.
He is the only one I fear. His noble spirit
Makes me feel less important.
That day we met the Witches,
They hailed him as father to a line of kings.
Upon my head they placed a crown,
But I have no son to give it to.
If the Witches are right, then
The crown will go to someone
Not descended from me.
I have murdered the gracious Duncan
Just for Banquo's sons.
I have destroyed my own peace of mind
Only for them. I have lost my soul

So that Banquo's sons may be kings.
I will not let this happen. Come, Fate.
We shall fight to the death.
(SERVANT *enters again, with two* MURDERERS.
To the SERVANT): Go,
Stand by the door until we call.
(SERVANT *exits. To the* MURDERERS):
Was it yesterday that we spoke?

MURDERERS: It was, your Highness.

MACBETH: Well then, have you thought
About what I said? I told you that it was
Banquo who betrayed you in the past.
You thought I was the one, but
You were wrong. It was Banquo all along.

MURDERER 1: You made it known to us.

MACBETH: Yes, I did. And we also talked
About something else, which is now
The point of our second meeting.
Do you think you can forgive Banquo?
Can you continue to wish him well,
After he almost sent you to your graves?

MURDERER 1: We are men, my lord.

MACBETH: Yes, you are called men.
So are hounds, spaniels, setters, and wolves
All called by the name of dogs.
Dogs' names tell what each dog
Is valued for. That way, we know which
Ones are fast or slow,
Which ones are hunters and which are pets.
The same is true of men.

Listen, and I will tell you about a plan
That will help you get rid of your enemy.
This plan will also put you in my favor.
I can only have true peace of mind
If Banquo, your enemy and mine, is dead.

MURDERER 2: My lord, I have been
So badly treated by the world.
That is why I don't care what
I do to spite the world.

MURDERER 1: The same is true for me.
My life has been full of disasters.
I would risk anything to make my life better
Or be rid of it.

MACBETH: Both of you know that
Banquo is your enemy.

MURDERERS: True, my lord.

MACBETH: He is mine, too.
We hate each other so much
That every minute he is alive is like
A sword thrust in my heart.
I have enough power now to
Sweep him from my sight forever.
Yet I must not.
Certain friends that are his and mine
Would not like it.
I cannot afford to lose these friends.
That is why I need your help.
You must do this deed for me,
But you must make it look as if
I had nothing to do with it.

MURDERER 2: My lord, we shall do
  What you command us.

MACBETH: Your spirits shine through you.
  Within an hour at most,
  I will tell you where you should go.
  I will give you exact instructions.
  This must be done tonight, and
  It must happen away from the palace.
  Remember that no one must suspect me.
  Don't fail in your mission!
  Fleance, Banquo's son, will be with him.
  It is just as important that you kill him, too.
  He must face the same fate as his father.
  Leave now, and make up your minds.

MURDERERS: They are already made up.

MACBETH: I'll give you further instructions
  Right away. Wait inside the palace.
  (MURDERERS *exit*.)
  It is arranged. Banquo, your soul's flight,
  If it will be to heaven, will be tonight.

(MACBETH *exits*.)

Scene 2

The palace. LADY MACBETH *and a* SERVANT *enter.*

LADY MACBETH: Did Banquo leave?

SERVANT: Yes, madam,
  But he will be returning tonight.

LADY MACBETH: Please tell the king
  That I would like to speak to him.

SERVANT: Madam, I will.

(SERVANT *exits*.)

LADY MACBETH: We have nothing.
    Everything has been done in vain.
    It would be better to be
    That which we destroy
    Than to live in such doubtful joy.
    (MACBETH *enters*.)
    How now, my lord! Why do you stay alone
    Thinking about what we have done?
    Your sad thoughts should have died
    With those whom you are thinking about.
    Forget about things you cannot change.
    What's done is done.

MACBETH: We have cut the snake,
    Not killed it. She'll close and be herself,
    And then she'll be able to bite us again.
    I would rather the whole universe fall apart
    Than continue to have the terrible dreams
    I have every night.
    Better to be with the dead, whom we,
    To gain our peace, have sent to peace.
    Duncan is in his grave.
    After life's fitful fever, he sleeps well.
    Nothing can hurt him ever again.

LADY MACBETH: Come, my lord,
    Stop thinking such foolish thoughts.
    Be bright and glad with our guests tonight.

MACBETH: I shall, my love.
    And so, I hope, will you.
    Let your words apply to Banquo.
    Show him special favor,

Both with your eyes and with your speech.
As long as we are not safe,
We must bathe our noblemen
In these flattering streams of words.
We must make our faces mask our hearts,
Hiding what we really feel inside.

LADY MACBETH: You must stop this.

MACBETH: My mind is full of scorpions,
Dear wife!
You know that Banquo and Fleance live.

LADY MACBETH: But no one lives forever.

MACBETH: And we can take comfort
In the fact that they might be attacked.
You never know. Before this night is over,
A dreadful deed shall be done.

LADY MACBETH: What's to be done?

MACBETH: You'll find out soon enough,
My dear. Later, you can applaud the deed.
Come, dark night.
Hide the tender eye of day.
With your bloody and invisible hand,
Tear to pieces the only thing
That keeps me pale with fright.
Darkness falls, and the crow flies
Into the woods.
Good things of day begin to sleep,
And night's dark agents find their prey.
I know you wonder about my words,
But be patient. Everything will work out.
So, I pray you, go with me.

(MACBETH *and* LADY MACBETH *exit.*)

Scene 3

A park near the palace. MURDERERS *enter.*

MURDERER 1: It's almost dark.
    They should be coming this way soon.

MURDERER 2: Listen! I hear voices.
    They must have left their horses with
    The grooms. I guess they wanted to walk
    The rest of the way to the palace.

(BANQUO *and* FLEANCE *enter.*)

MURDERER 1: It is Banquo and Fleance!

MURDERER 2: Let's get on with it!

(*They attack* BANQUO.)

BANQUO: Oh, no! Run, good Fleance!
    Run, run, run! Avenge me later! Farewell!

(BANQUO *dies.* FLEANCE *escapes.*)

MURDERER 1: We only got one of them!
    The son has run away.

MURDERER 2: We have lost
    The most important half of the pair.

MURDERER 1: Well, let's go
    And tell Macbeth how much is done.

(MURDERERS *exit.*)

Scene 4

A hall in the palace. A banquet is served.
MACBETH, LADY MACBETH, ROSS, LENNOX, LORDS, *and*
attendants enter.

MACBETH: You know where to sit.
　　To the first and the last, a hearty welcome!

LORDS: Thanks to your Majesty.

(MURDERER 1 *enters and stands at the door.*)

MACBETH: I'll sit down in a moment.
　　We'll have a toast to start off the meal.
　　(MACBETH *goes toward the door and speaks to
　　the* MURDERER.)
　　There's blood on your face.

MURDERER: It is Banquo's.

MACBETH: It's better on the outside of you
　　Than on the inside of him. Is he dead?

MURDERER: My lord, his throat is cut.

MACBETH: Good! What about Fleance?

MURDERER: Most royal sir, he escaped.

MACBETH: Oh, no! Except for this,
　　Everything would be perfect. As long as
　　Fleance lives, I feel boxed in
　　By doubts and fears. But Banquo is safe?

MURDERER: Yes, my good lord. He lies
　　Safe in a ditch, with 20 gashes on his head.
　　Each one was enough to kill him.

MACBETH: Thanks for that, at least!
　　There the grown snake lies.
　　The worm that has fled has no teeth yet.
　　We can deal with Fleance later. Go now.
　　Tomorrow we'll talk again.

(MURDERER *exits.*)

LADY MACBETH (*from the banquet table*):
　　My royal lord, you haven't given the toast.
　　If the host fails to welcome the guests,
　　The feast seems like one bought at an inn.

(BANQUO'S GHOST *enters and sits in* MACBETH'S
place, not seen by anyone.)

MACBETH: Dear wife!
　　Thank you for reminding me!
　　Here's to a good meal,
　　And good health to all!

LENNOX: Please sit, your Highness.

MACBETH: It is good to see our country's
　　Noblemen seated at this table.
　　If the honored Banquo were also here,
　　Our group would be complete.
　　I hope that his absence is due to rudeness
　　Rather than to an accident
　　That might have kept him away.

ROSS: His absence, sir,
　　Breaks his promise. Will it please
　　Your Highness to grace us with
　　Your royal company?

MACBETH: The table is full.

LENNOX: Here is a place saved for you, sir.

MACBETH: Where?

LENNOX: Here, my good lord.

(LENNOX *points to the seat where* BANQUO'S GHOST
is sitting. MACBETH *sees the* GHOST, *but nobody
else does.*)

MACBETH: Which of you have done this?

LORDS: What, my good lord?

MACBETH (*to the* GHOST): You cannot say
That I had anything to do with this.
Do not shake your gory locks at me.

ROSS: Gentlemen, rise.
His Highness is not well.

LADY MACBETH: Sit, dear friends.
My lord is often like this.
He has been since he was young.
Please stay seated. He will soon be himself.
If you notice what he is saying,
He will just get worse. Eat,
And pay no attention to him.
(*aside, to* MACBETH) Are you all right?

MACBETH: Yes. I am as strong as I must be
To look upon such an evil sight.

LADY MACBETH: What nonsense is this?
You are beginning to sound like you did
When you had that vision of a dagger.
You said that vision led you to Duncan.
You sound like an old woman telling
Stories by a winter's fire. Shame on you!
Why do you make such faces? When all
Is done, you are just looking at a chair.

MACBETH: No! Just look at him!
Can't you see him?
It is Banquo.

(BANQUO'S GHOST *exits.*)

LADY MACBETH: What are you saying?
   There is no one there.

MACBETH: I'm telling you the truth.
   I saw him.

LADY MACBETH: You're imagining it.
   Now, you'd better get back to our guests.
   They are beginning to wonder about you.

MACBETH: I almost forgot about them.
   (*to guests*) Do not worry about me,
   My most worthy friends.
   I have a strange sickness, which is nothing
   To those who know me. Come, love and
   Good health to all! I'll sit down now.
   Give me some wine, a full glass.
   (GHOST *enters again.*)
   I drink to the joy of the whole table,
   And to our dear friend Banquo,
   Whom we miss. I wish he were here!
   To all of us, and to him, we drink.
   Good wishes to all.

LORDS: We pledge our loyalty to you!

MACBETH (*to the* GHOST): Leave my sight!
   Let the earth hide you!
   Your bones are dead. Your blood is cold.
   You cannot even see out of those eyes!

LADY MACBETH: He gets like this sometimes.
   Do not worry about it.
   He'll soon be back to normal.

MACBETH (*to the* GHOST): Come to me like
   A rugged bear, a rhinoceros, or a tiger.

Take any shape but the one you have taken,
And my firm nerves shall never tremble.
Or be alive again and fight me
With a sword. If I hide at home, afraid,
Call me a baby. Get away, horrible Ghost!
Unreal sight, get away! (GHOST *exits*.)
At last! Now that you are gone,
I am a man again. Please stay away.

LADY MACBETH: You have ruined
The evening by acting so strangely.

MACBETH: Can such things happen,
And pass over us like a summer's cloud
Without having such an effect?
You make me think there is something
Wrong with me. How can you
See such things
And keep the natural ruby of your cheeks
While mine are white with fear?

ROSS: What things did you see, my lord?

LADY MACBETH: Please don't talk to him.
He grows worse and worse.
Questions make him angry.
Good night, everyone. Please go at once.

LENNOX: Good night. Better health
To his majesty!

LADY MACBETH: A kind good night to all!

(*All but* MACBETH *and* LADY MACBETH *exit.*)

MACBETH: What time is it?

LADY MACBETH: About midnight.

MACBETH: Why do you think Macduff
    Did not come to the banquet?

LADY MACBETH: Did you ask him why?

MACBETH: No, but I will find it out.
    Tomorrow, I will visit the Weird Sisters.
    They will tell me more. Even if I must use
    Terrible methods, I will find out
    The worst that the future holds for me.
    I am standing so deep in blood now.
    It would be easier to go in deeper
    And cross to the other side of this river
    Than to turn back at this point.
    I have strange ideas in my head,
    Which must be acted on.

LADY MACBETH: You need some sleep.

MACBETH: Come, we'll go to sleep.
    My strange vision of the Ghost
    Was just the fear of a beginner in evil.
    We are yet but young in deed.

(MACBETH *and* LADY MACBETH *exit.*)

Scene 5

The palace at Forres. LENNOX *and another* LORD
enter.

LENNOX: It seems that everyone who has
    Been close to Macbeth has suffered
        from it.
    Remember what happened to Duncan.

And brave Banquo, out walking at night,
Was killed by his own son, Fleance.
Fleance fled, so he must have been guilty.
Or so Macbeth would have us believe.
He also wants everyone to think that
Malcolm and Donalbain arranged
To have their own father killed.
Do you remember how Macbeth killed
Those two guards?
He said that they had killed Duncan.
Well, it was clear that those guards
Had had so much to drink
That they were dead asleep!
They couldn't have done it!
Macbeth must think we are all fools!
I think that if Macbeth could get hold of
Malcolm, Donalbain, and Fleance,
They would soon be dead, too.
I hear that Macduff is also out of favor
Ever since he missed that big banquet.
Do you know where Macduff is now?

LORD: He has gone to the English court.
    Malcolm, Duncan's son,
    Has been talking to King Edward.
    He has been trying to convince King Edward
    To get an army together to make war
    Against Macbeth. Macduff has gone to
    Help Malcolm tell Edward
    How bad it really is here.

LENNOX: I hope some holy angel
    Flies to the court of England with Macduff.
    And I hope a swift blessing
    May soon return to our suffering country.

LORD: I hope so, too.

(LENNOX *and other* LORD *exit.*)

Act 4

Macbeth visits the three witches and asks them about his future. They produce a series of visions, which tell the future in the form of a riddle.

After the witches disappear, Lennox arrives. He tells Macbeth that Macduff has fled to England. Angry about this, Macbeth orders the murder of Macduff's family. Murderers arrive at Fife, Macduff's castle, and kill everyone who is inside.

In England, Malcolm and Macduff make plans to restore peace in Scotland. They talk about the help that King Edward of England has promised them. Ross arrives with news about the murder of Macduff's family. This makes Macduff's desire to overthrow Macbeth even stronger.

Scene 1

A cave. In the middle, a large caldron over a fire. Thunder. The three WITCHES enter.

WITCH 1: Round about the caldron go.
  Into the pot, these things we throw!

ALL: Double, double, toil and trouble.
  Fire burn, and caldron bubble.

WITCH 2: Eye of newt, and toe of frog,
  Wool of bat, and tooth of dog,
  Tongue of snake, and lizard's leg—
  All go into the pot!

ALL: Double, double, toil and trouble.
  Fire burn, and caldron bubble.

WITCH 3: Scale of dragon, tooth of wolf,
Witch's mummy and poison plants.
Put them in the bubbling stew.

ALL: Double, double, toil and trouble.
Fire burn, and caldron bubble.

WITCH 2: Cool it with a monkey's blood.
Then the charm is firm and good.

WITCH 3: By the feelings in my thumbs,
Something wicked this way comes.

(MACBETH *enters*.)

MACBETH: Hello, you secret hags.
What are you doing?

ALL: A deed without a name.

MACBETH: I have some questions for you.

WITCH 1: Ask, and we shall answer.

MACBETH: I must know my future.
What is to become of me?
What am I to do?

(*Thunder.* VISION 1 *appears. It is a head*.)

VISION 1: Macbeth! Macbeth! Macbeth!
Beware the thane of Fife! Beware Macduff!
May I go now? I've said enough.

(VISION 1 *disappears*.)

MACBETH: Whatever you are,
I thank you for your words!
But I must know more—

WITCH 1: He is gone. Here is another,
Stronger than the first.

(*Thunder.* VISION 2 *appears. It is a bloody child.*)

VISION 2: Macbeth! Macbeth! Macbeth!

MACBETH: If I had three ears,
I would listen to you with all of them.

VISION 2: Be strong, bold, and firm!
You can laugh at anyone who fights you.
None of woman born shall harm Macbeth.

(VISION 2 *disappears.*)

MACBETH: Then live, Macduff.
I have no reason to fear you.
But maybe I'd better make certain.
You shall not live! That way, I'll be sure
To sleep in peace.
(*Thunder.* VISION 3 *appears. It is a crowned
child, with a tree in his hand.*)
What is this?
It looks like the son of a king,
With a crown on his head?

ALL: Listen, but do not speak to it.

VISION 3: Be fierce like a lion. Be proud,
And do not worry about your enemies.
Macbeth shall never lose a fight until
Great Birnam Wood
Moves to Dunsinane Hill
And fights against him.

(VISION 3 *disappears.*)

MACBETH: That will never happen.
Who could make a soldier out of a tree?
How could a tree pull up its roots

And march to Dunsinane Hill?
Sweet, good words! It appears that
I shall live until I reach old age.
Yet my heart wants to know one thing.
Tell me, if you know so much,
Will Banquo's children ever rule
In this kingdom?

ALL: Seek to know no more.

MACBETH: I must know. Tell me, or else
An eternal curse will fall on you!

WITCH 1: Show him!

WITCH 2: Show him!

WITCH 3: Show him!

ALL: Show his eyes, and grieve his heart!
Come like shadows, and then depart!

(*Out of the caldron comes a vision of eight kings and* BANQUO.)

MACBETH: You all look just like Banquo!
All of you have the same hair and eyes!
And the eighth one holds a mirror
In which many more are reflected.
And Banquo, spattered with blood,
Smiles upon me. He points at them,
And says they are his sons and grandsons.
(BANQUO and kings *disappear.*)
What? Is this true?

WITCH 1: Yes, sir. It is true. But why
Do you seem so surprised?
We told you about this a long time ago.

(*Music. The* WITCHES *dance, and then they disappear.*)

MACBETH: Where did they go?
    I hear someone outside the cave.
    Come in, whoever stands there!

(LENNOX *enters.*)

LENNOX: What is it, sir?

MACBETH: Did you see the Weird Sisters?

LENNOX: No, my lord.

MACBETH: Didn't they pass by you
    On their way out?

LENNOX: No, indeed, my lord.

MACBETH: I heard the sound of horses.
    Who was it that came by?

LENNOX: Two or three of us have come,
    My lord, to bring you some news.
    Macduff has fled to England.

MACBETH: Fled to England?

LENNOX: Yes, my good lord.

MACBETH (*aside*): From this moment on,
    When I have an idea about what to do,
    I shall do it right away. Even now,
    I have an idea for punishing Macduff.
    I will surprise everyone in his castle.
    I will give the edge of the sword to
    His wife and his children. After that,
    I will also kill all his unlucky relatives
    Who might be there at the time.
    I will not just boast about this like a fool!

I will order this before my anger cools.

(MACBETH *and* LENNOX *exit.*)

Scene 2

Fife. Macduff's castle. LADY MACDUFF, *her* SON, *and* ROSS *enter.*

LADY MACDUFF: Why did
My husband leave?
What was he thinking? Leaving Scotland
Makes him look like a traitor.

ROSS: You do not know if he left
Out of wisdom or out of fear?

LADY MACDUFF: Wisdom?
To leave his wife,
To leave his babies, and his home?
He must not love us. Even the tiny wren,
The smallest of birds, will fight the owl
To protect her babies in the nest.

ROSS: My dearest cousin, calm down.
Your husband is noble, wise, and brave.
He knows what is best for him to do.
I cannot say any more than this.
This is a cruel time, when our own king
Suspects people of being traitors
When they are not. My pretty cousin,
I must go. If I stay, I might start crying
About the situation you are in.
That would make me feel ashamed,
And it would make you feel uncomfortable.
So, I will go at once. (ROSS *exits.*)

LADY MACDUFF: My son,
    Your father is dead.
    And what will you do now?
    How will you live?

SON: As birds do, Mother.

LADY MACDUFF: How?
    With worms and flies?

SON: With whatever I can find, as they do.

LADY MACDUFF: Poor bird!
    You will be killed by the hunters!

SON: Why should I, Mother?
    Poor birds—birds of little value—
    Are not hunted.
    Anyway, no matter what you say,
    I know that my father is not dead.

LADY MACDUFF: He might as well be,
    For he is not here to protect us.

SON: Was my father a traitor, Mother?

LADY MACDUFF: Yes, he was!

SON: What is a traitor?

LADY MACDUFF: A traitor is one
    Who makes a promise
    And then breaks it.
    He promised to love and protect us,
    And now he has left. What will we do?

(*A* MESSENGER *enters.*)

MESSENGER: Bless you, fair lady!
    You do not know me, but I have come
    To tell you that danger is near.

Take my advice, and get out of here!
Run away with your children!
Heaven help you!
I do not dare to stay here any longer.

(MESSENGER *exits*.)

LADY MACDUFF: Where can I go?
And why should I run?
I have done nothing wrong.
(MURDERERS *enter*.)
Your faces frighten me. Who are you?

MURDERER 1: Where is your husband?

LADY MACDUFF: I hope he is in a place
Where you can never find him.

MURDERER 2: He is a traitor!

SON: You lie, you ugly villain!

MURDERER 2: What, you egg!
(MURDERER *stabs him*.)
You son of a traitor!

SON: He has killed me, Mother.
Run away, I beg you! (SON *dies*.)

(LADY MACDUFF *exits, crying "Murder!" She is
followed by the* MURDERERS.)

Scene 3

England. Near King Edward's palace. MALCOLM *and* MACDUFF *enter.*

MALCOLM: Let us find some dark shade,
And there we shall cry for poor Scotland.

MACDUFF: Crying will do no good.
Let us take our swords instead
And fight for our good country.
Each new morning, new widows howl,
New orphans cry, and new sorrows
Fill Scotland. It is all because of Macbeth.

MALCOLM: Just saying his name
Puts blisters on our tongues.
Macbeth was once a good man.
You have been loyal to him.
He has not hurt you yet.
Even though I am young, I know that
You may be using me to seek favor
With him. Maybe you will betray me—
A weak, poor, innocent lamb—
And give me up to Macbeth.

MACDUFF: I am not a traitor.

MALCOLM: But Macbeth is.
A good person may change when
Power is at stake. But I ask your pardon.
I have no reason to mistrust you.
Even though you left your wife and family
Without saying good-bye,
You must have had good reason.

MACDUFF: Thank you, my lord.
I would never betray Scotland
For all the power Macbeth holds.
I have lost my hopes for Scotland.
Bleed, bleed, poor country!

MALCOLM: Scotland weeps, it bleeds,
And each new day a gash
Is added to its wounds.
I think I can find people to
Help me get rid of Macbeth and
Put me on the throne of Scotland.
But, even if I did, the country
Would still be suffering.

MACDUFF: What are you talking about?

MALCOLM: I am talking about myself.
If I were on the throne, I would be even
More evil than Macbeth.

MACDUFF: No one could be worse!

MALCOLM: You are wrong.
You don't know me. The country is
Better off with Macbeth as king.

MACDUFF: Oh, Scotland! Scotland!
Unhappy country! My hope is gone!

MALCOLM: Macduff, I was just testing you.
I can see now that your love of Scotland
Is true. You have no plans to betray me
Or our country. What I said about myself
Was not true. I am a good and decent man.
I would rule Scotland well. Have no fear.
But why are you so silent?

MACDUFF: It's difficult to take all this in.
First you say you are not fit to rule,
And then you say you really are.
Give me a minute to think about it.

(*A* DOCTOR *enters.*)

MALCOLM: Well, we shall talk more later.
(*to the* DOCTOR) Is King Edward coming?

DOCTOR: Yes, sir. Many sick people wait
For him to cure them. His touch is holy.
He has been able to cure certain sick people
Just by touching them.

(DOCTOR *exits.*)

MACDUFF: What illness is he talking about?

MALCOLM: It is called "the evil."
Good King Edward is somehow able to
Cure those who have it. How he does it,
Nobody knows. But people who have
Big sores on their skin come to him.
He touches them, and they get better.
He must have a special gift from heaven.

(ROSS *enters.*)

MACDUFF: See who comes here.

MALCOLM: I can tell by his clothing
That he is from Scotland.
But I do not know him.

MACDUFF (*to* ROSS): Dear cousin,
Welcome to England!

MALCOLM: Oh, now I know who he is!
I have been away from Scotland too long!

May all that keeps me from Scotland
Soon change!

ROSS: Sir, I have the same wish.

MACDUFF: Is Scotland still like it was?

ROSS: Sadly, no. Poor country!
It can no longer be called our mother.
It is more like our grave.
Nobody there ever smiles anymore.
Sighs, groans, and screams fill the air.
Good men's lives end too soon.

MACDUFF: What can we do about it?

MALCOLM: What's the latest sad news?

ROSS: Anyone who tells what happened
An hour ago is hissed at.
Hour-long news is already old.

MACDUFF: How is my wife,
And all my children?
Are they still at peace?

ROSS: They were at peace
When I left them.

MACDUFF: Tell me more.

ROSS: When I was on my way here,
I heard stories that things in Scotland
Were just fine.
But I saw that the opposite was true.
Macbeth keeps on doing terrible things.
If we don't do something soon,
Our women will have to fight
To free themselves from his evil.

MALCOLM: We are on our way!
   The good King Edward of England
   Has given us 10,000 men to help us.

ROSS: I wish I had such good news.
   But I have words that should be
   Howled out in the desert air.
   There, nobody could hear them.

MACDUFF: What news do you have?
   Is it about all of Scotland,
   Or just about one person?

ROSS: The news is sad for everyone.
   But the main part of it refers to you alone.

MACDUFF: If the news is for me,
   Do not keep it from me. Tell me now.

ROSS: Do not hate me for what
   I am about to say.
   For I shall now tell you the worst news
   That you will ever hear.

MACDUFF: I can almost guess what it is.

ROSS: Your castle was attacked.
   Your wife and children were killed.
   If I tell you any more details,
   You couldn't stand it.

MALCOLM: Dear heaven!
   (*to* MACDUFF) Speak, man!
   If you don't talk about this,
   Your heart will break.

MACDUFF: My children, too?

ROSS: Wife, children, servants—

All that could be found.

MACDUFF: And I was not there.
My wife was killed, too?

ROSS: I have already said so.

MALCOLM: Dear Macduff.
Let us take revenge on Macbeth
For this terrible deed. In this way,
You can cure this deadly grief.

MACDUFF: But Macbeth has no children.
All my children are dead? Did you say all?
All my pretty ones, and their mother, too?

MALCOLM: Get revenge for this like a man.

MACDUFF: I shall do so.
But I must also feel it as a man.
I cannot stop thinking about those things
That were most dear to me. Did heaven see
What was happening, and not stop it?
It was all my fault, for I was not there!
May heaven take care of them now!

MALCOLM: Let your sorrow become anger!
Do not let it kill your heart.
Instead, may this grief sharpen it!

MACDUFF: If I could only cry like a woman
And take revenge like a man! Dear heaven,
Bring Macbeth and me face to face.
Place him at the end of my sword.
He would have no chance of escaping!

MALCOLM: Your words are brave.
Come, we shall go to King Edward.

We are ready. All we need is his nod.
Macbeth is like a ripe fruit on a tree.
He is ready to be shaken down.
Receive whatever cheer you may.
The night is long that never finds the day.

(All exit.)

Act 5

Lady Macbeth seems to have gone mad. Her doctor says he cannot help her.

Near Dunsinane, the forces led by Malcolm and Macduff get ready to attack. Malcolm orders his men to hide behind branches cut from the trees of Birnam Wood.

As he prepares for the attack, Macbeth receives the news that Lady Macbeth is dead. He also hears that Birnam Wood is moving toward Dunsinane. He is comforted by the words, "None of woman born shall harm Macbeth."

Scene 1

Dunsinane. A room in the castle. A DOCTOR *and* LADY MACBETH'S GENTLEWOMAN *enter.*

DOCTOR: How often does she sleepwalk?

GENTLEWOMAN: Since his majesty left
    For the field with the army,
    I have seen her sleepwalk every night.
    She rises from her bed, and then she
    Throws her robe around herself.
    She takes some paper, writes on it,
    Reads it, and seals it up.
    Then she goes back to bed.
    She does all this as she sleeps.

DOCTOR: This is not normal!
    Does she speak while she does this?

GENTLEWOMAN: Yes, but I do not dare
    To repeat what she says.

DOCTOR: You may tell me.

GENTLEWOMAN: I would not tell you
  Or anyone. I have no witness to
  Say I am telling the truth.
  (LADY MACBETH *enters, with a candle.*)
  Look, here she comes!
  See how she is fast asleep. Watch her.
  Stand close.

DOCTOR: How did she get that candle lit?

GENTLEWOMAN: She just picked it up.
  She has given orders to have light by her
  At all times. That was her command.

DOCTOR: You see that her eyes are open.

GENTLEWOMAN: Yes, but she cannot see.

DOCTOR: What is she doing now?
  Look how she rubs her hands.

GENTLEWOMAN: She always does that.
  She seems to be washing her hands.
  Sometimes she does it for 15 minutes.

LADY MACBETH: After all this washing,
  There is still a spot.

DOCTOR: Listen! She speaks!
  I will write down what she says,
  So I can remember it better later.

LADY MACBETH: Out, damned spot!
  Out, I say!
  Who would have thought the old man
  Would have so much blood in him?

DOCTOR: Do you hear that?

LADY MACBETH: The thane of Fife

Once had a wife. Where is she now?
What, will these hands never be clean?

DOCTOR: For shame, for shame.

GENTLEWOMAN: Heaven knows what she
Is talking about.

LADY MACBETH: Here's the smell of the
Blood. I can still smell it on my hands.
All the perfumes of Arabia will not sweeten
This little hand. Oh, oh, oh. (*She sobs.*)

DOCTOR: How she cries!
Her heart is full of sorrow.

GENTLEWOMAN: I would not want to be
In her place for anything.

DOCTOR: Well, well, well.

GENTLEWOMAN: Let us pray that
She gets well, sir.

DOCTOR: I do not know how to treat
Her illness. Yet I have known
Of people who walked in their sleep,
And later died with clean conscience
In their own beds.

LADY MACBETH: Wash your hands.
Put on your robe. Do not look so pale!
I tell you again, Banquo's buried.
He cannot come out of his grave.

DOCTOR: What is she saying?

LADY MACBETH: To bed, to bed!
There's knocking at the gate.
Give me your hand. Come, come.

To bed, to bed, to bed!
What's done cannot be undone.

(LADY MACBETH *exits*.)

DOCTOR: Will she go to bed now?

GENTLEWOMAN: Yes, right away.

DOCTOR: Terrible stories are being told
About evil deeds that have been done here.
She needs a priest more than a doctor.
God, God forgive us all! Look after her.
Try to be sure she cannot do herself harm.
So good night. What I have seen tonight
Was a great surprise to me.
I think I know what is wrong with her,
But I dare not say it.

GENTLEWOMAN: Good night, good doctor.

(DOCTOR *and* GENTLEWOMAN *exit*.)

Scene 2

The country near Dunsinane. Drums and flags.
MENTEITH, CAITHNESS, ANGUS, LENNOX, *and soldiers*
enter.

MENTEITH: The English forces are coming.
They are being led by Malcolm,
His uncle Siward, and the good Macduff.
The wish for revenge burns in them.
After what happened to them,
Even a crippled man would want to help.

ANGUS: We will meet them
Near Birnam Wood. That is the way
They are coming.

CAITHNESS: Will Donalbain be with them?

LENNOX: No, sir, he will not. I have a list
Of all the noblemen. Siward's son is there.
And so are many other young men
Who go to battle for the first time.

MENTEITH: What is Macbeth doing?

CAITHNESS: He is trying to keep his castle,
Dunsinane, safe. Some say he is mad.
Others, who don't hate him as much,
Say he is being brave. But it is certain
That he cannot go on for long.

ANGUS: He must know by now that
His secret murders are no longer secret.
Now, every minute, some small revolt
Reminds him of his own lack of loyalty
To Duncan. The people he commands
Obey him only because he demands it.
They do not do it out of love.
Now he must feel that his title
Hangs loose about him, like a giant's robe
Upon a small thief.

MENTEITH: No wonder he rules so badly.
All that is within him condemns
Itself for being there.

CAITHNESS: Well, we must march on
To give obedience where it truly belongs.
We shall soon meet the man who will
Save Scotland from this tyrant.

LENNOX: Yes, we shall.
Let us march now toward Birnam Wood.

(All exit, marching.)

Scene 3

Dunsinane. A room in the castle. MACBETH, *a* DOCTOR, *and attendants enter.*

MACBETH: Bring me no more reports.
 Till Birnam Wood moves to Dunsinane,
 I have no reason to fear.
 Where's the boy Malcolm?
 Was he not born of woman? The spirits
 That know the future have said this to me:
 "None of woman born shall harm Macbeth."
 So leave, false thanes.
 My mind and heart shall never sag
 With doubt nor shake with fear.
 (A SERVANT *enters.)*
 What is wrong with you?
 You look like a frightened goose!

SERVANT: There are 10,000—

MACBETH: Geese, villain?

SERVANT: Soldiers, sir.

MACBETH: Why are you afraid,
 You lily-livered boy? What soldiers, fool?

SERVANT: The English, your majesty.

MACBETH: Go away. Say no more.
 *(*SERVANT *exits.* MACBETH *calls his aide.)*
 Seyton! I am sick at heart. This battle
 Will probably mean the end.
 I have lived long enough. My youth is over.
 I am well into middle age.

That which should be a part of old age—
Honor, love, respect, many friends—
I will never have. Instead, I have men
Who obey me only because they fear me.
Seyton! Where are you?

(SEYTON *enters.*)

SEYTON: What is it, your highness?

MACBETH: Have you heard any more news?

SEYTON: All that was reported earlier
Has been checked and found to be true.

MACBETH: I'll fight, until my flesh is cut
From my bones. Give me my armor.

SEYTON: You don't need it yet.

MACBETH: I'll put it on anyway.
(*to the* DOCTOR) How is my wife?

DOCTOR: Her body is not sick, my lord.
But her mind is full of wild imaginings
That keep her from her rest.

MACBETH: Cure her of that!
Can't you heal her sick mind?
Erase her deep sorrow from her memory.
Get rid of the troubles written on her brain.
With some sweet medicine,
Can't you end the dangerous stuff
That weighs upon her heart?

DOCTOR: In such cases, the patient
Must heal herself.

MACBETH: Give medicine to the dogs!
I'll have nothing to do with it!

(*to* SEYTON) Come, put my armor on.
Send for my horses.
(*to the* DOCTOR) If you can, Doctor,
Find out what disease is troubling Scotland.
Make my country healthy again.
I will reward you well, if you can do it.
I will not be afraid of death and ruin
Till Birnam Wood comes to Dunsinane.

DOCTOR (*aside*): If I were away
From Dunsinane, free and clear,
No rewards could make me return here.

(*All exit.*)

Scene 4

Country near Birnam Wood. Drums and flags.
MALCOLM, SIWARD *and his son,* MACDUFF,
MENTEITH, CAITHNESS, ANGUS, *and* SOLDIERS
enter, marching.

MALCOLM: I hope the days are near
When people can sleep safely in their beds.

MENTEITH: We are sure that they are.

SIWARD: What is the name of this forest?

MENTEITH: Birnam Wood.

MALCOLM: Let every soldier cut a branch
And hold it in front of him. In this way,
We can hide our great numbers.
Macbeth's spies will make a mistake
When they count us.

SOLDIERS: It shall be done.

SIWARD: The only news we have heard is

That Macbeth is staying in Dunsinane.
He plans to fight us from there.

MALCOLM: That is his main hope.
The only ones who have stayed with him
Are those who are hoping for some reward.
All the rest have left him.

MACDUFF: Let's not judge those who
Stayed with Macbeth until after the battle.
For now, we should think of just one thing:
How we can be sure to win.

SIWARD: This important battle will decide
If Malcolm or the tyrant Macbeth shall rule.
Let the battle begin!

(*All exit, marching.*)

Scene 5

Dunsinane. Within the castle. MACBETH, SEYTON,
and SOLDIERS *enter, with drums and flags.*

MACBETH: Hang our flags
On the outer walls.
The strength of the outer walls and the
Inner walls will laugh at their attacks!
Let them lie in their camp outside our walls
Until they die of hunger and illness.
They are being helped by those
Who should be helping us. If not for that,
We would have been able to meet them
Face to face. We could have beaten them
With no trouble.
(*Women cry from within the castle.*)
What was that noise?

SEYTON: It was the cry of women,
   My good lord. I'll go see what's wrong.

(SEYTON *exits*.)

MACBETH: I almost forgot the taste of fear.
   There was a time that such a shriek at night
   Would have scared me. But now,
   After all the horrors I have seen,
   Nothing startles me.
   (SEYTON *enters again*.)
   What was the crying all about?

SEYTON: My lord, the queen is dead.

MACBETH: She would have died soon,
   In any case. But later would have been
   A better time for it.
   Tomorrow, and tomorrow, and tomorrow
   Creeps along slowly from day to day
   To the last moment of recorded time.
   And all our yesterdays have lighted fools
   The way to dusty death.
   Out, out, brief candle!
   Life is but a walking shadow.
   It is a poor player
   That struts and frets his hour on the stage
   And then is heard no more. Life is a tale
   Told by an idiot, full of sound and fury,
   Meaning nothing.
   (*A* MESSENGER *enters*.)
   What message do you bring?

MESSENGER: My Lord, I saw something,
But I hardly know how to report it.

MACBETH: Just say it!

MESSENGER: As I stood at my watch
Upon the hill, I looked toward Birnam.
I thought I saw the woods begin to move.

MACBETH: You are a liar!

MESSENGER: Be angry with me only
If it is not so. Within three miles of here,
You can see it coming.
I say, it is a moving grove.

MACBETH: If you are lying,
You shall hang alive upon the next tree,
Until you die of starvation.
If you tell the truth, I don't care
If you do the same thing to me.
I am beginning to wonder what the Vision
Meant when it said those words.
"Macbeth shall never lose a fight until
Great Birnam Wood
Moves to Dunsinane Hill
And fights against him."
And now a wood does come to Dunsinane!
Every man take up arms!
Go to your battle stations!
If this report is true, there is no use in
Running away or staying here.
Either way, it doesn't matter.
Ring the alarm bells! Come, ruin!
At least we'll die with our armor on!

(*All exit.*)

Scene 6

On the battlefield outside of Dunsinane.
MACBETH *enters.*

MACBETH: They have me surrounded.
    I cannot get away.
    Like a bear tied to a stake, I must fight
    Against the dogs who come to attack.
    What man was not born of woman?
    He is the one I must fear, nobody else.

(YOUNG SIWARD *enters.*)

YOUNG SIWARD: What is your name?

MACBETH: You would be afraid to hear it.

YOUNG SIWARD: No, I would not.

MACBETH: My name is Macbeth.

YOUNG SIWARD: Nobody could ever
    Say a name that is more hateful to my ear.

MACBETH: Nor could anyone say a name
    More to be feared.

YOUNG SIWARD: You lie, hated tyrant.
    With my sword, I'll prove it.

(*They fight, and* YOUNG SIWARD *is killed.*)

MACBETH: You were born of a woman.
    But swords I smile at, all weapons I scorn,
    If used by a man that's of a woman born.

(MACBETH *exits.* MACDUFF *enters.*)

MACDUFF: I heard a noise over here.
    Show your face, Macbeth!
    I want to be the one to kill you.

If not, the ghosts of my wife and children
Will haunt me forever.
Fate, let me find Macbeth!
I ask for nothing more than that!

(MACDUFF *exits.* MALCOLM *and* SIWARD *enter.*)

SIWARD: This way, my lord.
Macbeth must give up soon.

MALCOLM: Yes, it is true. His own people
Are fighting on our side.
They aim on either side of us,
Trying not to hit us.

SIWARD: Sir, enter the castle.

(*They exit.*)

Scene 7

Another part of the battlefield. MACBETH *enters.*

MACBETH: Why should I kill myself,
Just because we are losing?
I might as well take as many of the enemy
With me as I can.

(MACDUFF *enters.*)

MACDUFF: Turn and face me, Macbeth!

MACBETH: I have been trying to avoid you.
Please get back! My soul is too heavy
With your family's blood already.

MACDUFF: I have no words for you!
My voice is in my sword!

(*They fight.*)

MACBETH: You are wasting your energy.
    I live a charmed life. I will not be killed
    By any man who was born of a woman.

MACDUFF: Forget about your charmed life!
    Let the evil spirit whom you still serve
    Tell you this: Macduff was taken from
    His mother's womb prematurely.
    I was not born in the normal way.

MACBETH: A curse on the tongue that
    Tells me so! It has brought an end
    To my courage. I will not fight with you!

MACDUFF: Then give up, coward.
    We'll make you into a sideshow.
    We'll paint your picture on a board.
    Under it, we'll write, "Come in.
    Here you may see the tyrant!"

MACBETH: I will not give up,
    To kiss the ground before young Malcolm,
    Being hated by all. Though Birnam Wood
    Has come to Dunsinane, and you were not
    Born of a woman, I will still try my best.
    Come on, Macduff.
    I'll not be the first to cry, "Enough!"

(*They exit, fighting. Drums and flags.* MALCOLM,
SIWARD, ROSS, THANES, *and* SOLDIERS *enter.*)

SIWARD: It looks as if we have won,
    With very few losses.

MALCOLM: Macduff is missing,
    And so is your noble son.

ROSS: Your son was killed in battle.
　　He lived only till he was a man,
　　But like a man he died.

SIWARD: Then he is dead?

ROSS: Yes. He died bravely.
　　All his wounds were on the front.
　　None were on his back.

SIWARD. He died well. God be with him!

(MACDUFF *enters, holding* MACBETH'S *head.*)

MACDUFF: Hail, king! Behold this,
　　The tyrant's head. We are now free.
　　Hail, king of Scotland!

ALL: Hail, king of Scotland!

MALCOLM: You shall be rewarded well
　　For your bravery today. This dead butcher
　　And his evil queen are gone.
　　So, thanks to all at once and to each one.
　　Come and see me crowned at Scone.

(*All exit.*)